PROF. TWEEDLEDUM
NIMBUS CHUTNEY
PHD BS AMD

TWOURETTE'S, TWUMP, & TWEETS;
"THEY SAY, 'IT'S A PERFECT PERSONALITY'"

The untold story and Unreal
Nautobiography(TM)

Twourette's*,
Twump,
& Tweets

"'They say..... 'It's a Perfect Personality'"

The untold story and Unreal Nautobiography(TM)

by Prof. Tweedledum Nimbus Chutney, PHd, BS, AMD

with Dr. Jay Sordean, Pop-psychology Opinionista

Copyright 2020 The Redwood Clinic

*R45.307

TABLE OF CONTENTS:

ACKNOWLEDGMENTS

In keeping with the main character of this narcissistic, psycho-political thriller and academically scholarly breakthrough discovery announcement, the authors can only acknowledge one person. He who, without, this entire fabrication would not be possible or conceived of. Actually, it is more of a disavowing acknowledgement. Or meant to be.

SPECIAL NOTATIONS AND WARNING: This may contain content of a sensitive and potentially medically controversial nature. Do not attempt to self-diagnose yourself or others. Only rely on the expertise of a medical professional who you trust and who is qualified to opine on diagnoses and all matters medical. This is not intended to diagnose or offer treatment suggestions for anyone. The results described in this book are by no means usual or typical; they are not to be construed as results that anyone can achieve or rely upon now or in the future.

References to BANK Code and CodeBreaker Technologies are not attributable to BANK Code or CodeBreaker Technologies and they have no responsibility for the contents of this book. It is strictly the studied opinions and speculation of the author other than the decryption done by CodeBreaker Technologies AI system.

"I" Introductory Remarks and Raves About This Book: The preface

Why is "I" used to help describe the title of Twourette's in this Preface?

"I." The singular personal pronoun of the English language. Elegant. Singular. Standing tall like the egotistical (ego-testicle) pillar of stone called the George Washington Monument at one end of the reflecting pool in Washington, D.C.

"I." The EGO. Of course, this book in particular must begin with an "I" as it references the pinnacle personality, the perfect personality, which is the heart and mind of the subject of this book.

While loosely based on material stolen from the #2 bestseller <u>Donald Twump: Make America Gwait Again One Sound-Byte at a Time, The Real Nautobiography™</u> this emotionally impactful and sensationalistic psychomedical thriller white paper will over exceed your still stunted expectations of its value and relevance to your pitiable life.

Get over it! I'm just kidding.

The material wasn't stolen – it was acquired by legitimately contacting the copyright owner for permission to excerpt or copy parts of <u>Donald Twump</u>. While the author refused permission, we went ahead and cannabellized the contents whenever we felt like it.

Frankly, not much material was worth it from only a #2 Amazon bestseller. A bestseller, but not a #1 bestseller. Go figure.

Even if sued for infringement we would plead the fifth and temporary insanity – you'd have to be insane to use anything from a book that was not a #1 bestseller. Or at least some in the White House think so, as Number Two is nothing more than the first loser.

But perhaps insane is what the authors are, in thinking that this cutting-edge psychological breakthrough revelatory diagnosis of a politician/charlatan could wake up the masses who were mesmerized during the last Presidential election and actually cast votes for the ultimate electoral college winner of 2016. The person so commonly referred to as "he who cannot be spoken of," as if by mere mention of his (yes, this is a he) name would bring more evil to descend upon this fair nation.

"Twump Twump Twump Twump Twump Twump."

So there.

Now we've gone and done it. Uttered the name of what some consider to be evil incarnate. Well, if not evil incarnate, at least the champion bankrupter of companies and a nation. But he just couldn't help himself because that is what he is so good at. Many times over.

Now that the Corona Virus Panicdemic has overtaken the United States and the economic aftermath has been foretold to be the labeled the "Twump Depression," the authors of "Donald Twump" can say "I told you so."

At any rate, "Twourette's, Twump & Tweets" brings you, the reader, into a genre of literary work that has never existed before but needed to be birthed and dropped into this world awash in books and words.

And indeed it is the second in existence Nautobiography™.

Respectfully to the Reader,

Tweedledum M. Phinnius PHd, BS, etc. etc. and so on

(Great Uncle of the Author)

What Others say -- QUOTES and RAVES About this Epic

"Clearly 2020's best ever book to bestow upon your BFF." T.N.C.

"Sadly, this unabashedly leading venture of truth-telling and psychological torture and suspense will only reach #1 bestselling status on all of the book ranking charts. Number One is not good enough for a landmark work such as this." T.M.P.

"When I first read this landmark book, I was overtaken by an emotional catharsis no other book has ever moved me to. Clearly this will become the go to book in the esteemed halls of Psychological wisdom in community colleges and even Ivy League schools like Harvard, Yale, Princeton, Sarah Lawrence, Earlham, and Columbia." Sigmoid Freud, (posthumously)

"I wish I had lived to be able to read this book, endorse it, write the long forward to it like the Wilhelm Baines version of the I Ching, and elaborate on the subtleties of this pathology based in technology I never had the opportunity to see or use." Carlos Jung, (also speculative posthumous musings)

"Lies, lies, and more lies. Fake news. Fake psychology. Fake person. Make Psychology Great Again. They say..... I have a perfect personality. " D.J. Twump

"M" Melodramatic Preframing of this Book: Introductory remarks

Twourette Syndrome is a new DSM category created to match the pathology of the teens and 20's. The teens and 20's of the new century. The 21st century.

Most people know of the fairly rare but increasingly common disease or diagnostic category called Tourette Syndrome, or misspokenly called "Tourette's."

This is an organic brain condition characterized by tics (involuntary muscle twitches) and (not always) uninhibited blurting out of curse words and other usually "not socially acceptable" phrases during normal conversation. This is when words slip out – when out of nowhere the curse words come out. When the "executive function" of the brain doesn't control the deeper, more primitive parts of the brain. The mid-brain where the emotion-laden words come out naturally in an uninhibited fashion without a "reasoned and measured" censuring. The curse words are considered to be coming from the baser areas of the brain and coming from thoughts that lead to feelings which lead to an expressive behavior.

We are now in a new era in which the limitations imposed by online media platforms such as twitter have restricted the number of words or characters that can be spoken/written in a single message or missive. And these tweets have been limited now to 280 characters. This is double the 140 characters that was the limit up until mid-2017. The average number of characters in a English word in common speak is about 5 characters. So do the math. Tweets allow, on average, 28-56 words to shape a message. That tells you how much "cannot be spoken of." For the Tweetmeister, challenging to write unintelligibly.

 We have Twump in the White House, who we have crowned the Tweetmeister (in our previously published book, <u>Donald Twump</u>), who uses his Twitter account, the power of his tweets and the power of his Tweetheads-following to send out his vitriolic messages that seem like just purely stream-of-consciousness and unedited emotional tirades, attacks, barbs and cult-leader directives.

This is what we call Twourette syndrome (Twourette's), because it is based on Donald

Twump as the exemplar of this syndrome. This is the epitome of this behavior and psychological imbalance. Quoting Donald Twump, "They say…. it is a perfect personality." Twump's tweets are apparently spontaneous, uninhibited (and unspell-checked) and transmitted to hundreds of people at one time through the interspace. This is how, compared to the past, such languaging patterns can become implanted in the brains of so many so quickly like a corona-virus. Tweets transcend the social-distancing restrictions that prevent infection with bad RNA in already susceptible minds and hearts.

These uncensored verbages are not your garden variety epithets used by some people just as their normal speech patterns, lots of "F—K you," "Sh-t," " Sh---head," etc. etc. The kind of language that is called a curse word or potty mouth because it is not a highly elevated use of the English language or any of its derivations, such as American English, Australian, New Zealand, Canadian, or Indian-English (ex-Colonial, British Commonwealth related). After all, some would argue that of the tens of thousands of English language words to choose from, why do certain people use curse words or profanity every other word? Obviously, their self-esteem and social awareness is not pinned to the ability to be more selective in word choice. They choose to just speak from the mid-brain level of neurology vs the higher cortical regions. As if that were possible.

It is also curious to ponder this question, "Why do people who are supposedly "educated" revert to sixth grade level of vocabulary when they could easily choose 7th or 8th grade level words? Or even stretch to use high school graduate level language, let alone college level words at least every 3 paragraphs (if they graduated from college or at least can read a "college level" book)? Who knows?"

On the other hand, experts in mass-media communication are taught to dumb down concepts, don't use big words that people won't understand. That causes a disconnect, a lack of rapport. A break in the 3 second attention span so common nowadays. And so it is well known that most politicians and news casters use about 6th grade vocabulary to reach the common denominator.

Not to worry. That's a step above Sesame Street or Mr. Rogers. Wow. Such sophistication.

So, here we get back to the heart of this book.

Which is: languaging and psychology. Using short bursts of words to create emotion without the need for fact, detail, or specificity. The tweet in the hands of a Twourette Syndromer.

Reference: https://techcrunch.com/2018/10/30/twitters-doubling-of-character-count-from-140-to-280-had-little-impact-on-length-of-tweets/

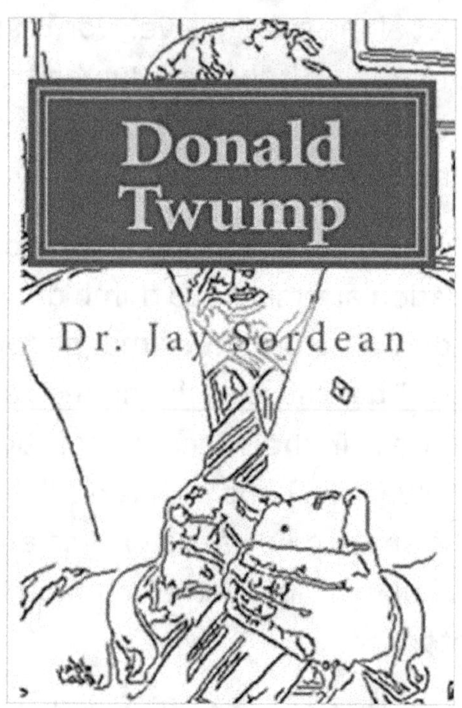

T Chapter 1 Tabloid Twump Turmoil

Aren't the tabloids a marvelous thing? An avenue to capture the attention of supermarket purchasers who are attracted to the salacious, the bizarre, the hyperbole, the fantasy, the fake story, the glitzy unimaginable life of the celebrities of cinema, television, radio, money, royalty, economic privilege, and social media.   The manufactured stories with perhaps a sliver of a fraction of a slice of truth buried under the fiction fantasy of vacuous rumor, gossip, and untruths. The historical underpinnings of so many phonies such as Donald Twump, and dare we confess, T.M. Phinnius.

Face Value & The Face-Value Quotient☺©

I guess it depends upon your background and many other factors, but whether you're skeptical or completely trusting can have an influence on your face-value quotient☺©.

We are all put in situations in life where we meet new people or people we already know and they will say something to us. Or they will say general statements. Or they will talk about somebody else. We hear it, we listen, and our brain typically immediately starts to interpret the information. Do we accept it as fact? Do we take it as the truth on its face value? Do we think, "oh, they are just joking," or "they are BS-ing us," or "that is a very intelligent thing to say," or "I never trust what they say," or etc., etc., and so on?

There are many factors that go into the ultimate interpretation chain in our brains.

We all know of certain people in our lives who we can say something to and they will seem to just take it at face value, whenever we say it. Now, we might be joking with them and they will catch on later. That is the kind of situation where it may be a harmless joke and we are both brought together more closely as a result of it. There are other times, when we know the person is "gullible," and we might exploit that gullibility in order to get something from them that normally they would not give us. We take advantage of the fact that they take us at "face value."

Then there are those of us who are skeptical and

suspicious of everything, and we can never really create relationships of trust and intimacy because we trust nothing. We take nothing and no one at "face value."

And then there are those of us, who have a mixture of trust and skepticism; and over time we develop the skills to apply those (trust and skepticism) appropriately in different circumstances so as to establish close ties with some people and to be wary or distance ourselves from others. Or at least, with those who constantly say things that we have come to know are unbelievable or just total hogwash, we will largely disregard what they have to say and categorize them as a fool or a liar, or a charlatan-like manipulator. Now we can only consider them a manipulator if what they say actually controls the thoughts and behaviors of either our self or other people. The words control inappropriately, and to the detriment of others.

This is essentially what happens in the presence of a sociopath, a narcissist, a perpetual-liar, someone who is unable to speak or recognize -- and does not care anything about -- facts or the truth. Are these people simply born that way or are they nurtured in such a fashion by parents and environment in order to, or just by happenstance, turn out that way?

Twump was born of the tabloids. He also fed them and they fed the celebrity status he craved. Tabloids are the "journalism" that Twump considers real, versus the fact-checking type of journalism he labels as "fake news." In his mind and based on his manipulation, fake becomes fact. Up is down. Wrong is right. Turmoil is constant. Take the lies and fabricated stories of the tabloids as the real Twump. Vacuous morsels describing the bon-bon substance of Mr. Turmoil Tweeting Twump.

Dare we take him at face value?

W Chapter 2 Winning and Whining, WIFM, Winner/Loser

Either you win or you whine about the person who won. It's always "what's in it for me" and there has to be a winner and a loser. There is no "win-win" allowed for a Twump.

Absolutely Absolutism

Absolute use of the word absolute, as in Absolut Vodka vs Smirnoff's

"ABSOLUTELY!"

It is completely undeniable that "ABSOLUTELY" is one of the most popular words going around and being used all the time -- on television, podcasts, radio, and politics. The certainty, the black and white quality and meaning of the word completely puts that word "absolutely" up along with the other words of the language, such as "never," "always," "without a doubt," "all the time," "forever," etc.

The issue here is that absolutes rarely exist in reality. But many people have a personality that wants to look at things as absolutes rather than as percentages. The gray tones or the 50 shades of yellow concept make them feel uncomfortable and confuse them. So they counter with the view that gradations are wrong. All things can be categorized as right or wrong, left or right, radical or conservative. A duality that all things concepts and behaviors fall into. Tolerance of "aberrant" behavior, as they define it, is unacceptable. There are rules and they must be followed (at least by others).

A great example of how persuasive these terms can be used is the rhetoric of Donald Twump. Read his tweets and you will find clear delineation of good vs bad. Things are divided by hard lines drawn in the sand or separated by fences. His conversations with Ukraine were "perfect." The Democratic party and impeachment hearings were all farce and scam. Nothing he does is illegal, immoral, or inexcusable. The mere fact that he is stating something or doing something makes it correct (in his eyes and mind).

Now this is more the result of narcissism rather than some moral or religious and legal principle. However, he couches his narcissistic behavior as beyond reproach and anything that is counter or objecting to his behavior is "evil" and a sham.

It is hard to believe that what he expresses on the campaign trail and in his "Presidential" speeches could be stated authentically and sincerely, but those who voted for him and who admire him seem to identify with what he says as if it were coming from the parted clouds of God. A white male God of course, but God nonetheless.

 These terms reference "no other possibility," "only one option," "absoluteism."

O Chapter 3 Orange Face

What about that orange face and orange hair he sports? Is it real or just fake and make up?

Not that make up is bad. It is used all the time by professionals in TV, cinema, acting, plays, the circus, dress-up events, Kabuki, Noh, San Francisco Mime Troupe, opera, symphony, musicals, and so on. All of those venues use cosmetic applications as a matter of course. They are used to achieve a particular effect. There is no harm in using such things. Even the <u>Hunger Games'</u> announcers had super make-up to create a greater-than-life persona and parody.

And what about that hair color too? Toupee or what? Orange?

Face-value Quotient☺©

It bears repeating: whether you're skeptical or completely trusting can have an influence on your face-value quotient☺©. But even more important is how much someone can trust what you say.

Your credibility is the key component on how high or how low your face-value quotient☺© is. Your face-value quotient☺© is what others interpret as how well they can believe what you say and how reliable your words (and actions) can be. The degree to which you tell the truth and the degree that you lie have huge influence on your face-value quotient☺©. And the face-value quotient☺© of others is the basis of the amount of effort you have to make in interpreting what they say as something you can believe "at face value" or whether you have to make an effort to really determine the truth of what is being said.

A pathological lier and someone you cannot believe at all has a -10 (minus ten) face-value quotient☺©.

Someone you can totally rely on and whose promises and statement are solid, without lies or falsehoods or fakeness, has a face-value quotient☺© of +10 (plus ten).

So what is the face-value quotient☺© of Twump? When you look at everything he has written, said and promised, objectively, you would have to say he is a -10. Minus 10. As low as you can get.

But you, the reader, might disagree. Some may say that what he says is true and anything contradicting that is fake news. Thus, some of you may say he is a +10. It is likely that you would be a Twump supporter and did in 2016 and will vote for him in November 2020. If you still believe him.

If not, well, we hope that is the case.

Frankly, how anyone could think that Twump's face-value quotient☺© could be anything but negative completely befuddles us. Fake face color, fake hair, fake celebrity, fake empathy, fake words, fabricated details, fake, fake, and fake.

A minus 10 (-10) face-value quotient☺© would be typical in the presence of a sociopath, a narcissist, a perpetual liar, someone who is unable to speak or recognize, and does not care anything about, facts or the so-called truth. You can't take anything they say seriously. It has to all be taken with, not simply a grain, but a whole spoonful of salt.

What other evidence bolsters this conclusion that Twump has a -10 face-value quotient☺©? What doesn't?

"Lier! Lier! Hair on Fire"

At least once a day someone comments on the lies and lying behavior of Donald Twump. There are books written on it. Other people routinely do fact checking of his words and those of his press secretaries and other staff members and find that either there are no facts or the facts contradict the statements.

According to Chris Cillizza of CNN, on June 10, 2019 "In his first 869 days as President, Donald Trump said 10,796 things that were either misleading or outright false, according to The Washington Post's Fact Checker. Do the math and you get this: The President of the United States is saying 12 untrue things a day...Trump is lying more every day than a majority of Americans wash their hands, according to data from the American Cleaning Institute."

https://www.cnn.com/2019/06/10/politics/donald-trump-lies-fact-check/index.html

Most would call this type of communication as lying. Others might excuse it and explain it away as a mistake, or erroneous, or a negotiating tactic. Like the way that all White House Press Secretaries are shown to do in the Twump administration.

A regular person on the street would more likely know the difference between the truth and a lie; between fact and fiction; between vacuous and substantive.

They should have at least the average ability to quickly discern the face-value quotient☺© of the speaker.

On the other hand, many people fall for the technique of repeating a lie over and over and over again – resulting in people believing it just because it was said by someone repeatedly. Here the listener has been mesmerized and entrained by repetition; the listener has been persuaded that the repetitive speaker has a higher face-value quotient☺© than perhaps they deserve. This is in spite of the fact that the lie-repeating person actually has a low face-value quotient☺©

Some personality types don't bother with details and facts. They will say anything off the top of their head just to win or convince others to agree with them or to do what they want them to do. A famous person from history was Adolf Hitler.

In the B.A.N.K. code personality system (www.Four-Cards.com to learn more), the ACTION type will bend the truth, or not even tell the truth, more often than any other personality type. Expedience, quick decision making and bullet-point information as the basis of primary behavior. Using fun, excitement, over-the-top emotional expression to motivate others to fall in line and agree. It is transparently easy to see this type of behavior through the tweets and press conference statements of Donald Twump.

Yet, is this excusable behavior for a President of the United States?

Granted, all governments and most politicians will tell lies or use omission of details and relevant information in their written and spoken communication. Spies, strategic misinformation campaigns, and other activities routinely employ lies and falsehoods to deceive the "enemy." Of course, when push comes to shove, the Twump administration will likely claim that all of the spontaneous tweets and scripted press conferences were intentionally spreading fake news for a higher purpose of national security or what have you.

From an ethical standpoint, is lying per se good or bad? What about when it is satire? In that case it is used for humor or comedy purposes. And that is a good. Some would argue that lying is good if it is a means to a good end. Others would say that it doesn't matter if the lie was used for a Win-Win outcome – the mere use of the lie is a bad thing. But most would think that the use of lies would depend upon how frequently they are used. If they are used constantly, that is a bad thing. If they are used rarely, they might be forgiven. Either way, the impact and significance of what is being lied about factors into this as well. If someone lies about an inconsequential thing, less or no harm. If someone lies (like the Enron scandal, Bernie Madoff, Donald Twump) and the lives of millions are negatively impacted, that is a more serious harm.

The fundamental conclusion is this: Donald Twump is a pathological liar and is very aware of what is a lie and what is not a lie. If for some reason he really doesn't know what the truth is and what is a lie, then he is mentally incapable of being President, no matter what the announced official opinion of his personal physician or the decision of the Electoral College.

U Chapter 4 Undiagnosed Diagnosis – Psychologists' comments over 5 years

From the beginning of the 2016 Presidential campaigns, starting in 2015, psychologists around the United States -- as well as arm-chair, amateur, and unlicensed psychologists and people who have taken any psychology class or read a book on psychology, have given their classifications of the psychological behavior and profile of Donald Twump. None have been particularly flattering diagnoses, unless of course you are a narcissist and anything that gives you more attention is a compliment. Narcissistic personality disorder, social pathology, pathological lier, early dementia, late stage dementia, bankruptcy-compulsive disorder, and the list goes on and on. There was even a document signed by about 200 professional psychologists warning the public of Twump's psychological stuff but apparently that never reached the desks of the faculty of the Electoral College.

So, as a result of all this conversation and debate, the author contemplated this plethora of opinions (professional and layperson), and had a revelation that might shake the foundation of the psychological professions around the world. It became clear, after finding an appropriate nickname – in the noble tradition of George W. Bush – that connected "the Donald" to Tweets (explained in detail in <u>Donald Twump: Make America Gwait Again One Sound Byte at a Time: The Real Nautobiography</u>™). It was inevitable that the subconscious mind would percolate up a new and refreshing diagnostic category linking Twump with his predominant behavioral and emotional characteristics.

Ergo, Twourette syndrome. The name of the new syndrome. Perfecto.

Et vois la!

For those who do not know of the reference manuals psychologists and psychiatrists and social workers and medical doctors and all other Western medical professions use for diagnostic labels and words, there is a book called the Diagnostic Statistical Manual. The DSM has evolved over the years and has various editions that are denoted by a number at the end of the DSM.

In this book we are referencing the DSM-5 codes. The fascinating story of creating the numerical code is told later in this book. We don't want you to get too ecstatic too quickly. Just hold on for another couple of riveting chapters.

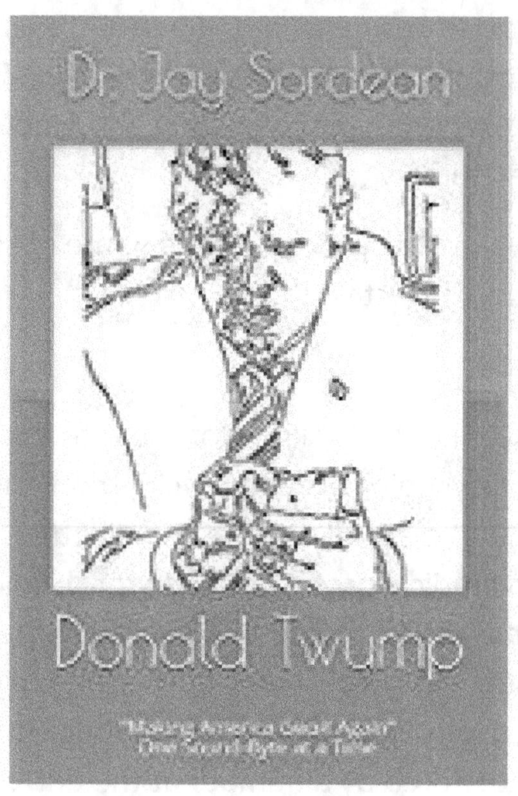

R Chapter 5 Revealing "the Perfect Personality:" A^4 (Action to the 4th power)

A Perfect Personality – Why is this in the title of this book?

"A Perfect Personality" is a twist on the well-known label that was uttered and repeated ad nauseum before, during, and after the impeachment of Donald Trump.

Of course, it references the "A Perfect Phonecall" label used to distort the true nature of the phone call. More accurately described by others as "a perfectly illegal phonecall," the now famous July 25, 2019 phone call, and possibly doctored transcript, was one element that led to the impeachment of Donald J. Trump.

Later in this book the phrase "A Perfect Personality," spoken tongue in cheek and in parody, will be elucidated. In other words, explained in more detail.

The Perfect Act - A charged Act – The ACTION^4
Type *

The DSM is a manual by the psychological professionals describing normal and abnormal/pathological psychological and personality types/categories/diseases/disorders/syndromes.

Personality types have been a fascination and source of inventive creativity by humans predating the written word. There are many systems developed, explained, and shared far and wide. They can be very instructive and helpful in grouping, classifying, understanding and predicting human behavior, thinking and anomalies.

A very powerful system is the BANK code personality system that has gained fame and legitimacy over the last couple of decades since its creation by Cheri Tree. There are four defined types as described in her book "Why They Buy BANK." If you are curious as to your own "configuration" please play the four cards by going to www.Four-Cards.com and play the cards, complements of the coauthor.

This system was applied to the 2016 presidential campaign by the coauthor in the number one bestselling book "Code Blue in the White House: What Successful Presidents Sell Voters to Win Elections." The four basic types are described briefly in that prescient suggestor of the outcome of the election. The most important conclusion, that has remained consistent year after year, is that Donald Twump's BANK code is ACTION type. Not only that, everyday people's perception, no matter what country they are from, is that he is almost exclusively ACTION, and very little of any other card type is evident in his personality or persona.

Now there are a very small percentage of people, like maybe 5%, who choose other cards as his primary type. These typically are people who state that they are big supporters and love Twump.

Given the statistical predominance of spontaneous, virgin thinking by world citizens about these four personality types with respect to Donald Twump, I conclude and concur that Donald Twump is an ACTION-ACTION-ACTION-ACTION (namely ACTION^4) personality type.

Unique? Yes.

Rare in the purity of his personality manifestation? Yes.

Consistent enough to qualify for a moniker of "A Perfect Personality?" Yes.

Perfectly (undiluted) ACTION type?

Statistically significant enough to go into the Diagnostic Statistical Manual? Absolutely.

And as a bonus, the authors consider him to be the perfect case study for those learning the "One World, One Language" BANK code personality system. We might even call it (him) a "gift from heaven." Well, let's not get carried away with too much praise (although ACTION types feed on that enormously – it gives them the attention that they crave and makes them feel even more like a winner).

Ergo, the unassailable and undeniable association of ACTION[4] with NPD and Twourette syndrome. The person with an ACTION[4] personality is also a specimen revealed when their Emotional Intelligence is extremely undeveloped and unmanifest in behavior, thought, attitude, and feeling.

***AUTHORS NOTE and DISCLAIMER: This is the opinion of the author and in no way represents or is anyway associated with BANK, BANK code personality system, or any of the principals or officers or Certified Trainers or any and all others related to any offshoot or company associated in the past, present or future of Codebreaker technologies, or any other names that they may choose in the future.**

E Chapter 6 Executive Action – Tweets, Executive Orders, Fire-Ready-Aim

Managing a company requires a team effort even when there is a strong leader at the top. Delegation of authority is typically a skill that is needed to get all the many pieces of a successful enterprise to work. It demands communicating vision, policy, plans, and actions requires finesse and consistency.

The Government of the United States is no exception. The President is something like a CEO, and the attitude and style of the CEO affects the operation of the organization. While there are 3 branches of the US government, the White House has a lot of power. And not just power in how the health and well-being of the United States will turn out. We are talking about global stability and environmental protection or destruction here.

There are many types of personalities that exist in the world. Some are meant to be leaders who can bring people together, others are not suited nor inclined to operate in that manner. The loose cannon, the perpetual disruptor mentality, the person who is an admirer of being a dictator-CEO ends up creating chaos. Expressing and showing loyalty and "yes-man" behavior is the only way people under the CEO retain their positions and jobs. Or it leads to practicing deviously and constantly looking over their shoulders.

It is said that quick decision makers want an executive summary and decide based on a few bullet points. Instead of having things prepared and laid out clearly in advance, they will shoot first, see what happens, make corrections, and shoot again. The "shotgun" or "machine gun" approach. This is the opposite of the "ready, aim, fire" typical instruction given to people learning to do new things, in particular learning to shoot an arrow or fire a bullet from a gun. The latter approach is often also necessitated when there are limited resources and you only get one chance to get it right. Like as a sniper. Or a hunter with limited arrows. Or a hungry human in the desert.

Fire, (Ready), (Aim). That is exactly how Twump has governed in the White House and how he has always operated his businesses before the White House. He is known to act quickly, firing staff members who did not do what he said. At the same time it is likely difficult knowing exactly what one was to follow is hard because contradictory statements spew forth from the Donald even in the same sentence.

That this would happen was adequately predicted various places, included in <u>Code Blue in the White House: What Presidents Sell Voters to Win Elections (2016)</u>. This quick trigger behavior was evident before his ascension to the Oval Office and has been commented upon untold times by those who dealt with, and still deal with him directly.

Senator Bob Corker is just one example who was beleaguered by Twump's lying and erratic behavior, as reported October 17, 2017 in a summary of his interview with CNN. Another Republican who was dismayed and not fooled or blinded by the personality of Twump was Senator Jeff Flake. His speech announcing plans to retire and calling on Republicans to reject President Donald Trump's "flagrant disregard for truth and decency" when addressing the president pro-tem of the Senate is highly instructive and eloquent. It is a recommended reading for everyone.

When CEO of his companies, Donald Twump could create the rules and change the rules at his whim. That is how he has chosen to run the White House and the country. This is in spite of the oath to "uphold the laws and the Constitution of the

United States." When he can't get his way legislatively, he writes an executive (dis)order. More often than not those orders are flawed in some way and have to be rescinded or significantly re-worded. Fire, Ready, Aim.

In the employment arena a common adage is "hire slowly, fire quickly." In other words, find the best person for the job, but if they don't work out or are a bad fit, don't let them stay around as they will destroy the company. "Cut bait."

Based on this philosophy taught even at Wharton and Haas, there must be a rather complex process that is involved in the hiring of people to work with Twump. Those going in have to know that they follow in the pathway cluttered with discarded predecessors. What is the preparation manual they are given by those who recommend them? What tricks are they clued into to retain their dignity, their integrity, and then -- last of all -- their job? What else can the secret employee manual say other than repeating, chapter after chapter, "suck up to the Chief" and then "leave gracefully when you head is offered you on a platter?"

From what anyone on the outside can observe, in the Oval Office there is no Ready and Aim when it comes to his White House staff hires. It is simply Fire. And Fire again. And Fire again.

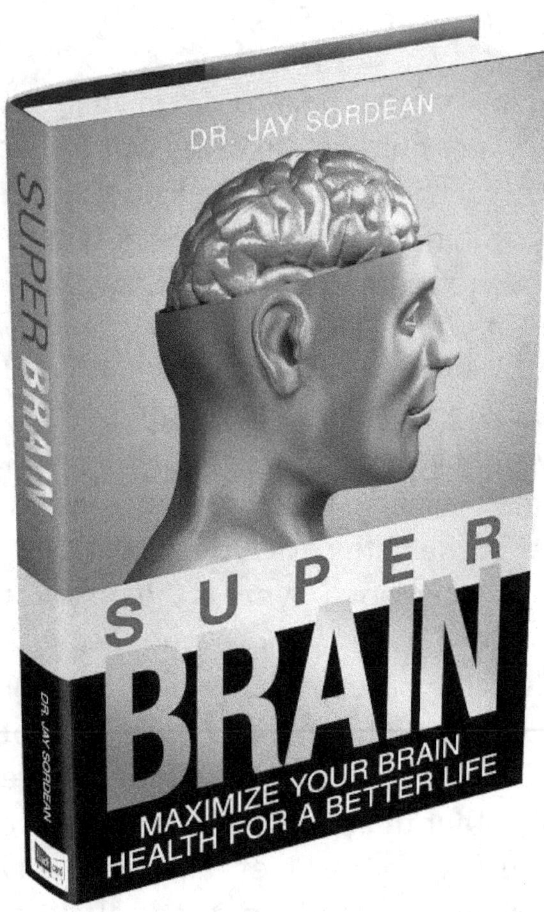

Superbrain-thebook.com

T Chapter 7 Twourette Syndrome

What you are about to read may be the most frightening and disturbing thing you have ever pondered. I do not advise that you continue if you are faint of heart or weak of mind. It may torment you in your sleep and cause you to question the sanity of those around you, those in the media, and those in the White House.

This chapter contains the secrets of the psyche that very few have studied, let alone understood. So if you are still with us at this point and haven't closed the book, venture forth with caution and an open mind, as this may lead you to an entirely new outlook on life as you know it.

Most people know about the very rare, but increasingly popular, psychological condition called Tourette syndrome.

This particular condition is considered to be an organic brain syndrome where curse words or other words that are culturally inappropriate are used without restraint and spontaneously by a person in conversation. Note that this is different from the deliberately curse-word laden routines by some comedians and others with full conscious control. And it differs from the standard Tourette's syndrome in which only about 10% have uncontrolled cursing along with their tics.

But here we talk about something even more deadly, more mysterious, more…one might go so far as to say, dubious. A thing called Twourette Syndrome.

While we have created a code for Twourette Syndrome to fit it in the DSM, it is unlikely that it will become an official code and diagnosis in that esteemed and yet ever-changing manual. In this chapter we will define what Twourette's syndrome is and how it resembles its well-defined uncle, Tourette's Syndrome.

Tourette's syndrome was named after the physician who first "discovered" and labled it, Gilles de la Tourette. According to **Dr. Barbara Coffey, MD, MS & Maxwell Lubelt,** only about 0.3-0.5% of the population worldwide has Tourette syndrome. On the other hand, it is important at this early junction to clarify that this newly defined phenomenon, Twourette Syndrome, applies to only one person on this planet at the current moment. Namely, Donald Twump.

Nevertheless, just as other "named" diseases or conditions are named after the discoverer of the condition, or were at least identified by that person, a derivation of the name of a disease can be modified to meet the current needs of medical and psychological science. Disease, syndrome, or disorder names can come from a case study or a series of cases someone studied as part of a medical practice. Indeed, this is a new category that comes from a particular individual who has made that tweeting style a trademark and a brand. It is also his brand, his primary vehicle to communicate with the world. It also seems to be the primary hallmark of the thinking and feelings expressed by that individual.

Defining Criteria / Symptoms: The condition of Twourette Syndrome is a compulsive production of tweets filled with fake facts, put-down statements about others, dismissive missives purporting to point out the weaknesses of others, lacking -- any remorse, self-reflection, admissions of mistakes, apologies, or any other suggestion of imperfection.

The tweets contain qualities of fabrication of non-facts, narcissism, vitriol, misogeny, racism, homophobia, legaloidish drival, and pompass bellicosity. These Twourette (aka Twumpian) tweets are also devoid of detail and rather contain generalities, non-specifics and simplistic phrases that are circular and written at about a 3rd grader's level of language.

The 6 "V's." Another quick diagnostic tools to spot Twourette is the vocal and written appearance of the following: vapid, vacuous, vicious, vatriputive, voracious, and valueless utterances.

<u>How does Twump stand up in the competition to be number 1 on Twitter?</u>

As of July 29, 2019 at 7:06 AM PST, @realDonaldTrump had 43.2K Tweets, 62.4 Million followers, 47 following

Hillary Clinton
11K Tweets 24.9 million followers

Don King
25.9K Tweets

Bernie Sanders
14K Tweets 9.4 million followers

Joe Biden

2,170 Tweets   3.6 million followers

Kamala Harris

11.5K Tweets 3 million Followers

Barack Obama

15.7K Tweets 107.4 million followers

Elizabeth Warren

5,161 Tweets 2.9 million followers

Kirsten Gillibrand

18.8K Tweets 1.4 million followers

Marianne Williamson

16.4K Tweets   2.7 million followers

Pete Buttigieg

9,267 Tweets 1.3 million followers

Cory Booker

64K Tweets   4.3 million followers

The Late Show: Stephen Colbert

23K Tweets 728.7 K followers

ヴェネティス

37.8M Tweets 42.6 followers 0 following

According to Carl Bialik, on the 10th anniversary of Twitter in March 2016, the most prolific tweeter was "@VENETHIS with 37.771 million tweets. He has 43 k followers. He's in first place by a lot, ahead of the second-place account by almost 31 million tweets. He has posted more than 15,000 tweets per day since joining Twitter in August 2009." (https://fivethirtyeight.com/features/the-worlds-most-prolific-twitter-user-tweets-mostly-about-nothing/)

As of 7-29-19 that number had risen to 37.8 million. Only 29 thousand more in 3 years.

But still, the Donald has a long way to go to be number 1.

Donald Twump is not number one in Tweets. He has simply defined a whole new category of psychological syndrome based on tweet behavior. And he can boast that he is the winner in that category, he is Number One for Twourette syndrome.

NPD (Narcissistic Personality Disorder) DSM-5 301.81

Narcissistic personality disorder (NPD) is a personality disorder with a long-term pattern of abnormal behavior characterized by exaggerated feelings of self-importance, an excessive need for admiration, and a lack of empathy. People affected by it often spend a lot of time thinking about achieving power or success, or about their appearance. They often take advantage of the people around them. The behavior typically begins by early adult hood, and occurs across a variety of social situations. (from Narcopath.info)

The Amazing Story of Discovering the DSM-5 code of Twourette Syndrome

When a new psychological code is created, (I assume) the number it is labeled with has to match up with other similar categories. So in this case, let's start with a list of DSM-5 codes of relevance to peak your interest and set the stage for the rather boring logic associated with final creation of the code number.

308.3 Acute stress Disorder

307.52 Eating disorder - pica

307.23 Tourette syndrome

305 Tobacco Use

304.52 hallucinogen dependence

304 Cannabis dependence / drug addiction

303 Alcohol dependence

301.81 Narcissistic personality disorder

R45 (ICD-10) Restless and agitation

Given that numerous psychologists have publically labelled Donald Twump, among other things, as NPD (narcissistic personality disorder) we chose that one – 301.81 – as a landmark, a starting point, in creating a diagnostic code for Twourette in the DSM.

Also, because Tourette is 307.46, we looked for an empty number that was halfway in between. Halfway would be 304.52. However, that number was taken by "hallucinogen dependency." This in and of itself is an interesting idea that Twourette would be associated with some habit of relying on hallucination (are you thinking "alternative" or "fake reality"). While there was temptation to just stop and just choose an already taken category, we fought attention deficit disorder behavior and persisted on.

So, after choosing to use the DSM-5 of 307.96, that converted into R45, R45 being taken from another classification system used in medical coding. The International Coding for Diagnosis, ICD. ICD-10 to be exact. Restlessness and agitation combined into the code 307.

We expect that you are following along carefully the step-by-step process of mathematically and psychologically coming up with a new numerical code for Twourettte Syndrome. Based on all of this explanation, and calculated through our proprietary and secret algorithm to come up with new codes, we logically, and intuitively, settled on the code "**R45.307**."

So that's how we got R45.307 as a NEW CODE for a new diagnosis, Twourette syndrome.

Twourette Syndrome. A new DSM psychological category. R45.307

And, many of you already caught this. The unconsciously competent choice of the number 45. Not Colt .45, but Oval Office occupant number 45. Makes sense and it's thus an easy number for doctor's to remember as well.

Add Years to Your Life
BRAIN WEALTH
Secrets
And Life to Your Years
AS SEEN ON
CBS NEWS
FOX
NBC
abc
Dr. Jay Sordean, OMD
Clinician, Educator, Speaker
Best-Selling Author

T Chapter 8 Tourette Syndrome

By now, you probably already know a lot about Tourette Syndrome from the last chapter.

Don't you think Twourette Syndrome is more interesting than Tourette?

If so, just skip ahead to the next chapter and forget about Tourette Syndrome.

On the other hand, if you really want to know about Tourette Syndrome you can go look it up on the internet.

But we recommend the better option. Just now move on to the next to the last chapter of this landmark document.

E Chapter 9 End Game – Survival & Big Money Comeback

Some have said that Trump never expected to win the election. And yet he did.

Besides his huge ego, need for a phone that lenders would answer, need for an avenue to do bigger real estate deals, why else did he run for the White House? Speculation runs rampant, so let's let it run rampant again. Tabloid style.

This chapter includes an as-of-yet-unpublished op-ed piece written 24 January 2020, prior to the Senate acquitting Twump of consequences of impeachment by the House. By none other than our opinionista.

"Violating the Constitution Under Penalty of Death"

Op-Ed Piece by Dr. Jay Sordean January 24, 2020

In 2017 people asked me my thoughts on why Donald Twump wanted to be President and what was going to happen. Based on my understanding of his history, I first said that we have to look at "what's in it for him." Essentially because, while everyone has some self-interest in everything they do, that is especially the case and always the psychological and motivational underpinnings of Donald Twump.

So what else did I say? Given his string of bankruptcies, his lack of lenders picking up the phone when he called, and his need to go to Russia and elsewhere for his business capital, becoming President would give him a new status – no one would refuse to answer his calls. As we all know, when the President of the United States calls, you pick up the phone.

Secondarily, becoming President also puts one in the seat of a vast intelligence network that can help find new real estate opportunities. Like building golf courses in a transformed North Korea for pennies on the dollar.

With another 3 years of observation of Donald Twump's actions and behaviors, I now see another even deeper motivation for him to remain President by whatever means necessary – beyond the obvious egotistical testosterone-oriented reasons speculated above.

Fear of death motivates many people to take extraordinary measures. He is no exception to the rule.

Let's say that you are massively in debt to organized crime, and organized crime has threatened to kill you and your family if you do not pay back what you owe. Certainly, this is a story that humans have heard across the centuries as well as have seen and hundreds, if not thousands, of movies and television shows in the United States and abroad.

This scenario does exist in real life so, let's assume the story of a person who borrowed lots of money to begin and sustain businesses. Then, bankruptcy after bankruptcy has found him in (or rather, put himself into) a position where his usual commercial lenders in New York City and elsewhere were no longer willing to throw good money after bad again. So this individual -- still owing money , perhaps also to gangster interests in gambling cities such as Atlantic City and Las Vegas -- has to then search outside of the borders of the United States, in greater amounts than previously already done, and ended up finding willing oligarch lenders in Russia or elsewhere.

Now let's also assume that these transactions are largely "off the book" and taking place in international business corporations around the world. It will come as no surprise that much of commercial business, and political donations, are done in this economic banking and discreet business transaction arena. However, that does not mean that they are not real and that the debt owed is not obligated it to be repaid in one fashion or another. The borrowed money is real, taken seriously by the lender, and required to be paid back, with terms, by the borrower.

So now, let's say that that same individual, whose almost singular skill is creating bankrupt businesses, suddenly finds himself unable to pay back the new and current debt or the funds that had been borrowed from these new powerful forces.

Perhaps, he is cornered into a situation where the only way out, in lieu of unavailable cash payments on the debt owed, is to do something else. With a little bit of discussion, the solution to the debt dilemma is to run for President of the United States. All he initially has to do is run for the presidency.

Now, his creditor/lenders are investing in a "political IPO," a newbie, a novice to Washington politics, a "disruptor" so to speak. If he loses at least he has disrupted the U.S. political status quo. If he wins, "AHHH," sweet opportunity to really create and provide creditors some serious payback.

So he takes actions that will compensate the lenders for their current losses. And becoming President is in total alignment with his own psychological megalomaniacal ideations. He runs for president and somehow, with their help, he does become President of the United States.

Now, this lacky and shill - whose family's and personal life was under threat due to defaulting on his loans, has created the perfect situation as far as protection of himself and his family. Worldwide and 24/7, he now has a private security guard system called the Secret Service. The security detail of numerous agents is constantly there -- protecting his life with their own lives. And of course, paid for by the taxpayer. Nothing out of his pocket again. A free ride. Just like the string of bankruptcies in the wake of his supposed (assumed) and self-professed business acumen. Using the universal vehicle for wealth and riches – OPM (other people's money).

What else is "perfect" about this? A presidential "private security guard" advantage continues to be provided after leaving office. Yet, this bodily security is not absolute or guaranteed. It is possible to circumvent the protective powers of the Secret Service, as has been shown in numerous situations through the course of American history where presidents were attacked and even assassinated.

The bottom line is this: Donald Twump has achieved all of his goals: 1) seeking public office, not for the sake of anyone else - like to serve the American public - but merely to protect his own body and feed his ego, 2) to make as much money as possible in real estate through the advantage of secret information (and private meetings with dictators behind closed doors) paid for by the US taxpayer that only certain eyes have an opportunity to see, and 3) to feed his narcissistic ego by being in the limelight constantly.

All of the intelligence briefings and the status of the office of the President are major tactical and strategic advantages the President has at his fingertips. Donald Twump will literally do anything to keep that going as long as possible.

And with impeachment proceedings, you can imagine how frightening this is for an individual whose life and the lives of his family members, are under constant surveillance by his lenders. Lying is not above his pay grade.

The final key question is, if impeached and forced from office, does he continue to have his salary, protection by the Secret Service, and continued access to leaders and dictators worldwide?

His Presidential salary in and of itself puts him in the upper 3% of income brackets in the US, perhaps notwithstanding his massive indebtedness otherwise. If impeached, is he stripped of salary and Secret Service protections? If so, perhaps we can have some compassion for a man and his family that will be put in greater threat of bodily harm by creditors. But, it takes a much bigger person than I am to worry about the consequences of that man's words and actions.
© 2020 Dr. Jay Sordean

AFTERMATH of OPT-ED PIECE

The above op-ed piece was written prior to the Senate hearings on Impeachment of Twump. Given that the Senate did not support impeachment removal of Twump from office, Twump retains his lifetime of Secret Service protective services. He wins taxpayer-paid (this is socialism, folks) security guards, a pension for life, access to daily briefing on the most top secret files of the country (insider trading information), and many more perks (like personal connections with multiple numbers of dictators who he can cut real estate deals with). He gets it all, while the economy for many will be failing them still, 4 years later, even if he loses the 2020 election. This is <u>not</u> a job that you get paid based on accomplishments or productivity. (Just because you did a bad job doesn't mean you lose reelection.)

Not only does Twump get all of the above benefits, he now even has a psychological pathology named specifically in his honor, another #1 win. That is a first. No other President has that distinction. Twump is an all-time winner!!

S Chapter 10 Summary – The Executive Summary

And for, they say it's a perfect personality, the A^4, we provide bullet points; we now give you the coveted, and required by the ACTION decision maker, an....

EXECUTIVE SUMMARY

- Trump + Tweets = Twump
- Twump + Tourette = Twourette
- Twourette + White House = Twurmoil
- Twurmoil = Title of the next book.

ABOUT THE AUTHOR

Tweedledum Nimbus Chutney is a fictional non-fiction writer based internationally (and nowhere in particular) and a pen name for Finnius Bandersnatch, a charlatan and envious Presidential-wannabe, who is also charading as a celebrity reality TV CEO, and masquerading as a wolf in sheeps dungerees. She is available for keynote speaking engagements costing more than fees demanded by past Presidents and dictators. Contact agent for booking.

The primary author's degree designations were bestowed posthumously to another obscure author and then the rights were purchased to add to authority and legitimacy to this epic scholarly work of genius inventivenss. Nevertheless, her degrees, born of pseudo-academic humility in the face of an egotistical world awash in pseudo- and amateurish writer aspirees, include the AMD (almost medical doctor), BS (bullsh--ter), and PHd (piled higher and deeper). She is more famously known as the great niece of the unknown ghostwriter psychiatrist Tweedledum M. Phinnius. TMP is not properly credited for having written the great psychological revelatory works by Erickson, Freud, Jung, Chuang Tze, Lao Tze,

Buddha, Orman, Dr. Phil, Oprah, Will Shakespeare and others of greater or lesser significance.

ABOUT THE POP-PSYCHOLOGY OPINIONISTA

Dr. Jay Sordean has co-authored numerous unpublished and published books, often co-authored with himself. [This, in and of itself, raises some psychological question marks which will not be addressed either now or in the future.]

As far as being a premier opinionista goes, "They say" that Dr. Jay's pop-psychology opinions rival those of his

rivals and that his perhaps?-Midwestern-derived sense of "humor" is vastly underrated and completely misunderstood by 99%, or even more, of the English-speaking population in the multiverses.

(Author's condescending yet necessary clarifying note for the geographically challenged: The "multiverses" actually includes the Earth.)

Dr. Jay's qualifications in the psychological realm are more than some and less than others, deriving from decades of observation, study, reading, classroom, clinical, personal experience, interpersonal conversations, group conversations, internal conversations, group therapy, couples therapy, individual therapy, rebirthing therapy, and processes both conscious, sub-conscious, unconscious, and supra-conscious.

The same can be said of Tweedledum Nimbus Chutney and her Great-Uncle, T.M. Phinnius.

<u>Other highly significant and compelling books you can buy now on Kindle and Amazon include:</u>

- ✓ "Outsmarting the Dementia Epidemic" (2014)
- ✓ "Super Brain: Maximize Your Brain Health for a Better Life"(2014)

- ✓ "BRAIN WEALTH SECRETS: Add years to your life and Life to your Years"(2020)
- ✓ "Code Blue in the White House: What Successful Presidents Sell Voters to Win Elections(2016)"
- ✓ "Donald Twump: Make America Gwait Again One Sound Byte at a Time: The Real

Nautobiography™"(201
7)

✓ "Code Red in the White
House: Turmoil in the
Presidentiality©: Five
Years of Trump Chaos
and Dictator-Envy©: 10
more years to
go?"(2020)

✓ https://www.amazon.com/Outsmarting-Dementia-Epidemic-Alzheimers-Successfully-ebook/dp/B00TFS5PBC

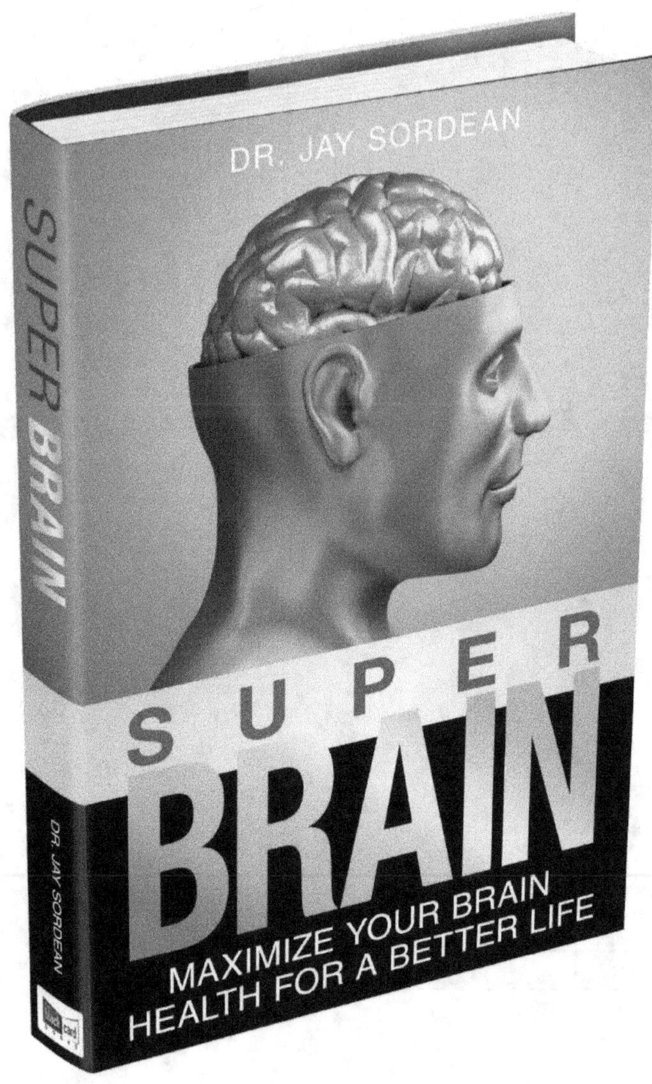

✓ https://www.amazon.com/Super-Brain-Maximize-Health-Better/dp/1514734362

https://www.amazon.com/BRAIN-WEALTH-SECRETS-Years-Your-ebook/dp/B087F6WGF3

✓ https://www.amazon.com/Donald-Twump-Making-America-Sound-Byte/dp/1520913982

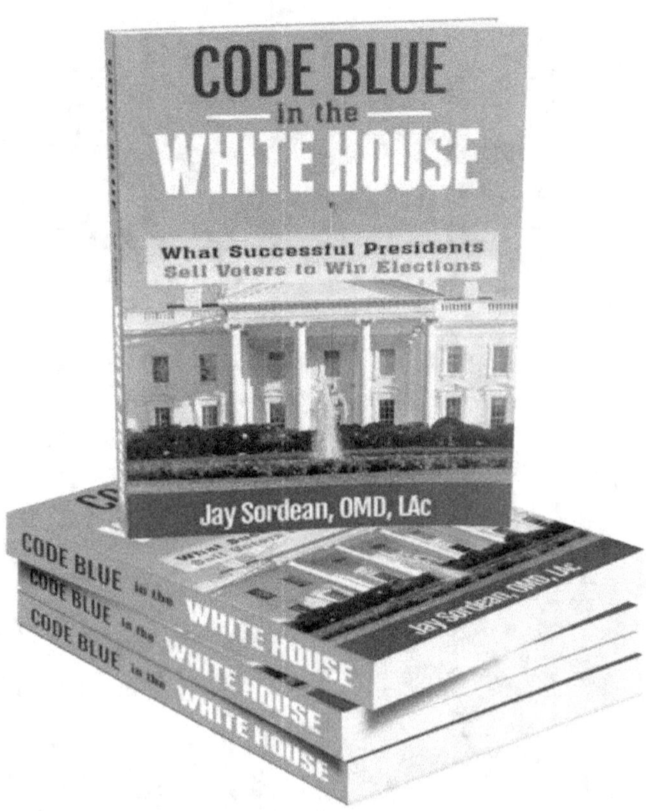

✓ https://www.amazon.com/Code-Blue-White-House-Successful/dp/1537155660

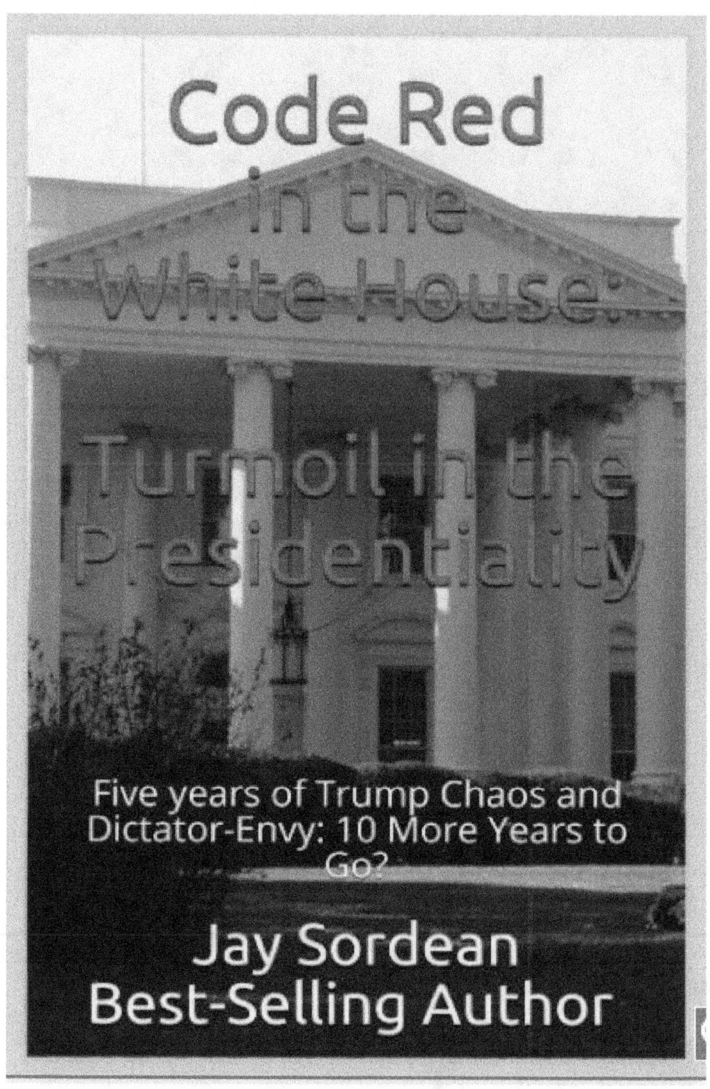

✓ https://www.amazon.com/Code-White-House-Presidentiality-Dictator-Envy/dp/B08928L659

SPACE FOR READERS' NOTES, COMPLAINTS AND CRITIQUE: R45.307

"& may #46

replace #45

in 2020"